NAVIGATING ASSISTED LIVING

THE TRANSITION INTO SENIOR LIVING

KRISTI STALDER

ISBN-10: 1-7324558-0-5

ISBN-13: 978-1-7324558-0-1

Visit the author's website at www.KristiStalder.com

First Edition: February 2019

STALDER BOOKS & PUBLISHING, LLC

Acknowledgements

I wish to acknowledge with gratitude, Stephen Lalonde, Amy McGarry, Kim Verdone, Mary Koch, and my mother for their help and support during the writing and editing process of this book.

A special acknowledgement to my former colleagues Roxy Ahlskog, Shari Pasco, Chelsey Steely, Shannon Kokkinen, Danyel Currier, Lorna Ottmar, Lani Cruz, and Heather Salerno.
Your beautiful hearts are the lifeblood that makes assisted living exceptional for so many seniors. Thank you for making such a positive impact in my life.

Finally, I lovingly acknowledge my husband, Bert.
You taught me the power of a successful mindset, and put the wind back into my sails. Thank you for being such an inspiration.
I love you more than life itself.

Contents

Introduction

No Regrets

Age is inevitable. Aging isn't.
—Marv Levy

I STOOD ON THE BOW OF A FERRY off the Seattle shoreline late one evening. The moment was perfect; my boyfriend had just given the most beautiful proposal speech, and I cried tears of happiness while he slipped a diamond ring onto my finger. Amid the high of this euphoric moment with the dazzling city lights before us and the sound of water lapping against the ferry as we glided across the Puget Sound, my cellphone chimed in my pocket. I snuck a peek at the screen to see that it was a text message from Susan, the daughter of an elderly couple I'd been working with during their transition into assisted living back home in

Spokane. At a glance, I could tell that it was urgent. Susan was furious about an incident with her parents that had occurred at the facility.

Ten minutes later, my phone chimed again. And again, and again. I quickly apologized to my fiancé and excused myself. He gave me a strange look, and I assured him that it was an emergency and I would be right back.

I dialed Susan's number, and she answered on the first ring.

"Kristi," she growled, "I want to know what is going on at that facility!" She was seething, and before I could say a word, she unleashed her anger with a list of complaints. My heart sank as she continued, "Mom called me and said that nobody has been to her room, and she pushed her call-button a half hour ago! And the staff said they couldn't give Dad his pills out of his pill organizer? Why not? I don't understand why they can't just do it, because that's what he's used to," she went on, and on, without letting me speak. "I'm starting to regret this move, Kristi, and I want some answers."

Susan's parents, Clayton and Bertie, were settling in. It was their second night at the assisted living facility. In the weeks prior to the move, I had gotten to know this couple and their daughter, and my perception was that Susan was much more apprehensive about the move than Clayton and Bertie. She had a preconceived doubt about the staff's ability to keep Mom and Dad safe, and she fretted about changing their daily routine from what they were used to. Her parents, on the other hand, were a bit anxious but pleasantly confused and overall content to be in their new home.

I apologized profusely. There was a possibility that Bertie forgot to use her call-button, or perhaps there was an emergency with another resident, or maybe the staff hadn't responded yet. Without being at the facility to investigate, I could only speculate. I tried to explain that the state regulations prohibit the staff from dispensing medications without an order from the doctor, but as I spoke, I could almost feel her anger seeping through the phone. Susan didn't want to hear me talk about regulations. She didn't want to hear about the limitations to the personal care that she assumed her mother would receive. Susan's anger arose from a misconception of what assisted living truly was.

Eventually, the situation was diffused, and we agreed to meet when I returned to the office. I ended the call, and sat for a moment, collecting myself. I thought about what I could have done differently to ensure that Susan and her parents understood the service they were buying. I didn't realize how little she understood about the process. I'd shown her the amenities in the apartment, and we discussed the types of services that we could provide, but I didn't tell her what to expect after the transition. I didn't warn her of the cognitive decline her parents may experience during the first thirty days, or that it will take a few weeks for the staff to learn Mom and Dad's routine preferences. I failed to explain exactly how the staff responds to emergencies, and what would happen if additional personal care services were required.

Admitting these mistakes is difficult, but it gave me the opportunity to create something and avoid a similar situation from happening to someone else. There are a few books and resources about assisted living, but the literature only scratches the surface of what assisted living entails. I want you to be prepared and know exactly what to expect during this life-changing transition. I don't want you to have any regrets about the transition, either.

As the former business office manager and admissions coordinator at an assisted living facility in Spokane, Washington, I have over a decade of experience working with thousands of seniors and their families, all of whom were seeking a solution to their loved one's unsafe living situation. During those years, I learned and followed the procedures within the senior living industry, specifically financial and accounting, admissions, and administration. This knowledge has been used to help medically compromised adults find a safe environment that would enrich their quality of life. It was my job to provide information and the resources necessary to make their decision to move easier, and to guide them through the entire process. I did so with a passion.

The book you're reading was inspired by Susan's situation and the phone calls from desperate family members seeking guidance for their loved ones. Many of the conversations were similar and had two things in common: no one knew where to start, or what to expect.

As it's true for many, the transition into senior living is no longer a choice. Instead, it becomes a necessity in order to thrive. Unexpected events may force the decision of who accepts responsibility to care for your loved one, and you may feel like you're lost, unsure, and overwhelmed.

So where do you start? How are you supposed to facilitate this and carry on with your own busy schedule? How are you or your loved one going to manage this, financially? How will you suggest to your loved one that they must move into an assisted living facility, and what will you do if they refuse to cooperate?

Everyone's circumstance is different, and the dynamics of events leading to your inquiry vary, but the underlying issue is all the same. When your loved one cannot live independently due to a health or safety concern and becomes a hazard to themselves or others, you must make some difficult choices on their behalf. Rest assured, no matter how impossible the situation may seem, there is usually a way to resolve it.

It's easy to go onto the computer and Google questions about senior living, and you'll find dozens of websites that can tell you all about it. I've pulled many of the resources about assisted living together and added the critical information from my experience to create this guide.

Each state has different rules and regulated assisted living practices. To maintain accuracy, this information is general in nature, and projects what an average assisted living facility provides to get you started in the right direction. Remember to check with the facility that you're inquiring about and confirm the services, amenities, policies, and procedures that I am describing.

If you are already familiar with the beginning process of finding an assisted living facility, this may offer a different perspective and enable you to find comfort in knowing that your situation may not be so different from the rest, and you are not alone.

Let's begin this journey together, and I'll help guide you along the way.

Chapter One

Why Assisted Living?

You may delay, but time will not.
—*Benjamin Franklin*

THE CRITICAL ELEMENT TO SUCCESSFUL aging relies heavily on the need to recognize when assisted living becomes necessary.

When a car begins to show signs of a problem, a mechanic will troubleshoot to locate the cause. Similarly, with the aging process, as we begin to present signs of a physical or cognitive issue, the doctor will troubleshoot our symptoms and determine the complication. It may be something simple that can be resolved with an adjustment to the diet or an antibiotic. Or, it could be a permanent issue and require the help of professionals to manage, thus leading to a recommendation for assisted living. The point is: if our bodies or minds aren't functioning as well as they once did, and we begin to make mistakes that endanger ourselves or someone else, there is a medical reason and it shouldn't be ignored.

When the time comes and the doctor declares that Mom will thrive in an assisted living facility, it's best to follow their recommendation.

Determining the right environment to ensure safety is ultimately in your loved one's best interest. Many families hesitate to seek out assisted living because of the cost, and they end up selecting a housing option that will accommodate their loved one's basic needs for only a short time. Emotions play a significant factor in this decision process, and in the beginning, denial is at the forefront of our minds. No one wants to accept the fact that Dad has dementia and thinks someone is sneaking into his house to eat his ice-cream, no matter how hard you try to convince him that it's not logical, and he just forgot that he ate the ice-cream. It is so important to stay focused on your loved one's best interest and to avoid feeling guilty when it's time for assisted living. Remember that your decision is ensuring an improved quality of life for Mom or Dad.

Not only does their quality of life improve, but yours does, as well. By moving your loved one into an assisted living facility, you are granted the peace of mind knowing that they're going to be taken care of around the clock and that someone is there to respond to emergencies. Additionally, your loved one will enjoy other benefits such as social activities with other residents, and they'll make friends with seniors who share common interests. You will have comfort knowing that they'll be eating three meals a day, all of which is approved by a dietician and balanced. Not only that, but the continuous medical and health monitoring and communication from the staff and doctor lifts a weight from your shoulders because trained professionals will address health concerns as they arise. You can return to your role as the family member, and not the caregiver. It enables you to enjoy your loved one's company, and not resent being around them, as you are granted the freedom to spend quality time with them while maintaining their dignity.

TIMING IS CRUCIAL

Let's talk about dignity.

As our loved ones age, they begin to lose bodily functions. The loss of those functions can turn into a disaster in public, in front of company, and at home. Expecting our loved ones to maintain personal hygiene when it becomes a challenge is not helpful. It is our duty as family to protect their dignity and promote safety after recognizing the decline in practicing good hygiene. When accidents become more frequent, the safety risk increases with many factors. As with bladder and bowel incontinence, the presence of bacteria when not appropriately cleansed can cause urinary tract infections (UTI), which are common with the elderly. These infections create complications such as increased falls, confusion, and the person could potentially become septic. Sepsis is a life-threatening condition that is caused when bacteria from an untreated UTI spreads into the bloodstream.

Another hazard of incontinence includes skin breakdown in those hard-to-reach places, which lead to open sores or infections. Remaining hopeful that our impaired loved ones will clean themselves properly after an incontinent accident is another risk and another disaster waiting to happen.

Assisted living facilities provide the services to maintain resident dignity and ensure safety. The care staff will provide hands-on assistance with changing briefs, perineal care- also known as "peri care" (washing the genitals and anal area). They will watch for sores and skin breakdown and recognize when the integrity of the skin becomes weak or compromised. If so, they will communicate with the doctor for instructions and apply topical prescriptions to protect the area before it can get any worse.

When these types of hygiene problems present themselves, it is an indication that action must be taken to prevent your loved one from unintentionally harming themselves. It's an uncomfortable subject to discuss with your loved one, and it may take some creative words of encouragement to influence good hygiene practices and avoid offending them. Try using phrases such as, "Let's go freshen up before we head out!" You'll find that your loved one will be more receptive to a suggestion phrased as such, and chances are you will have the opportunity for a pleasant conversation about getting them some help. I've found it useful to say, "let's go..." as opposed to "you should go..." or "you need to...". This suggests that I am involved and willing to help with whatever the task may be. Adults don't like to be told what to do, rather, a suggestion and polite words of encouragement will do the trick.

Timing is everything; don't wait until it becomes a medical emergency. The sooner you can recognize the need for help, start looking into safer options for them.

WHAT, EXACTLY, IS ASSISTED LIVING?

Not to be confused with skilled nursing, rehabilitation, retirement or independent living; assisted living is a housing facility that provides assistance to seniors 55 years or older with activities of daily living (ADLs). These are tasks such as dressing, bathing, toileting, maintaining bowel or bladder continence, and transferring in and out of bed or chairs.

It's the step in-between living independently and living in a nursing home. Those who are medically compromised and need some extra help with daily life can sign up for a wide range of ADL service levels. The type of service and frequency depends on the resident's cognitive ability, safety awareness, and mobility. Within an assisted living facility, staff members perform various functions to assure residents' safety.

Caregivers, or certified nursing assistants (CNA) complete state-specific required training courses to provide care to the residents.

The medication technician (med-tech) dispenses physician-ordered prescriptions to the resident at the directed times and with directed doses. It is the med-tech's responsibility to ensure medications are refilled when necessary and the dosages are updated when the resident's doctor writes an order.

Oversight of the nursing department is provided by the health services director. He or she is ultimately responsible for all of the residents' health and wellness.

Depending on the size of the facility and number of residents, an assisted living will employ a team of various directors including housekeeping, maintenance, dietary, activities, admissions, and an administrator.

Assisted living facilities have private rooms or apartments. The average accommodation includes a small kitchenette with a refrigerator and microwave, a full-size barrier-free bathroom with a walk-in shower, and a small living space equipped with pull cords for assistance within the room. Some facilities will provide a pendant or button in addition to the pull-cord station for the resident to use as a means to call the staff for help.

Assisted living facilities will usually offer housekeeping, maintenance to the apartment and grounds, social activities, outings, and transportation to and from medical appointments. Keep in mind that all facilities operate differently depending on which state you live in and may not offer the same services; some are complimentary, or the facility may charge a fee.

There are a few terms to familiarize yourself with as you begin your search. Often, you will hear "assisted living facility" and "skilled nursing facility," or "ALF" and "SNF." The difference between them is a skilled nursing facility provides temporary housing and care with goals of rehabilitation and cognitive/physical improvements, so the patient can recover from an injury or illness and return to their former living situation. An assisted living facility is a permanent housing establishment where the goal is to maintain the resident's cognitive and physical level by assisting with ADLs until the resident declines and is no longer safety aware and becomes a hazard to themselves or others. For a senior to be considered appropriate for assisted living, he or she must be stable and predictable. Stable, meaning their health cannot fluctuate rapidly, rendering them unable to call for help. Predictable, meaning they will not be at risk to wander and get lost.

INDEPENDENT & RETIREMENT LIVING

You may be familiar with the terms "independent living" and "retirement living." These facilities are significantly different from assisted living or skilled nursing, particularly because they do not include nursing oversight. If a medical incident were to happen to a resident in an independent living facility, he or she would not have access to medical staff and would need to call 911 for help independently. It's a common belief to think that some seniors will thrive in an independent living facility because it may offer some amenities such as prepared meals, housekeeping, and other non-ADL services. In reality, choosing the wrong environment could create an even bigger problem for your loved one and ultimately become a factor in rapid health decline.

Independent living and retirement facilities are tempting because they're significantly less expensive than assisted living. Up to several-thousand-dollars-a-month less. Independent living is an option for seniors of sound mind and body. Bear in mind, your loved one will continue to age and may need to make another move with further health declines. Is it more appropriate to locate an assisted living facility, even though your loved one is still somewhat independent? Ask yourself these questions when considering an alternative:

- ✓ How long do you predict that they will remain independent before needing some extra help?
- ✓ Does their current diagnosis suggest complex medical issues or an upcoming surgery?
- ✓ What would happen if they fell inside the residence and could not get up?
- ✓ Will inclement weather affect their safety?

Most independent living facilities are non-subsidized and private-pay only; therefore, your loved one will be paying out of pocket. It may not seem like an issue at first, but if the time comes and Mom needs to transition into assisted living, but she does not have sufficient funds to sustain the rental payments, she would need to apply for Medicaid. That's where things can get complicated and create some significant financial obstacles. Most assisted living facilities have a minimum two or three-year private pay requirement before accepting Medicaid as payment. If there is a sudden need for assisted living, she could be placed on a year-long wait list for the next available Medicaid apartment.

Be sure to review all financial avenues to determine what your next step should be. Document your loved one's account balances and asset values, and establish the current available funds. Consider any debt and factor the number of payments until the balance will be paid in full. Include all income sources, such as Social Security or pensions. Once you have narrowed down a monthly budget with the current balance information, you can estimate how long the resources will cover the cost of rent and services. Specific costs will be determined after you contact a facility, but you will need to know this information beforehand. If you discover that the available funds will not cover the cost of rent and services for at least a year, begin to familiarize yourself with the Medicaid application process, which I'll explain in the next chapter.

Some independent living facilities have a buy-in option. There are pros and cons to ownership versus renting, and the commitment can offer a long-term benefit of connecting with the community. Communities that offer buy-in apartments or houses typically have a continuum of care services on the campus, known as a Continuing Care Retirement Community, or CCRC. This allows for the resident to age in place, and take advantage of the additional services as needed, and they can use the money from the buy-in to cover the costs of an increased level of care. Use caution when considering a buy-in, as the flexibility to move out when health requires is not offered. An investment indeed, but a sudden health emergency can send Mom to a skilled nursing or rehabilitation center for an extended length of stay, and depending on the severity of the diagnoses, she may not have the option to return to independent living. The results are costly, and often the resident ends up paying for both locations while they recover. Every facility has its terms and conditions, and it is imperative to understand the process of releasing the buy-in investment or refunding the entrance fees and deposits. It might be an excellent option for someone who is financially and medically stable, but a sticky mess for those who are not prepared.

IN-HOME CARE AGENCIES

A temporary solution to providing help while living at home or independent living would be to employ a home care agency to provide one-on-one assistance. Typically, these services are not covered by insurance. Fees are charged hourly with a minimum-hours requirement per service call.

This type of assistance is recommended if your loved one is recovering from an illness, or if they are feeling under the weather and need some extra help with things such as meal preparation, errands, housekeeping, and medication reminders. The home care agency staff will assist until your loved one recovers and no longer needs help. Most agencies will continue to reach out and follow up to maintain the relationship so that your loved one will employ their services in the future.

Using these services is not a living arrangement, but a short-term solution to an immediate medical issue. It also subtly introduces the idea of accepting assistance if the individual is reluctant or in denial about aging. Home care agency staff will offer companionship services for those suffering from depression or loneliness and can make the transition easier by showing your loved one that it's okay to ask for help.

SKILLED NURSING & REHABILITATION

For many seniors with a complex medical history, a visit to the hospital will frequently be followed by a short-term stay within a skilled nursing and rehabilitation facility. It is considered a step-down from hospitalization, and the senior has the services of medical staff as they recover from recent surgery or an illness. Some facilities are furnished with private and semi-private rooms and somewhat resemble a hospital setting. Seniors will receive assistance from a team of nurses and care staff, and a house doctor will provide oversight throughout the recovery process.

The average length of stay in a skilled nursing and rehabilitation facility depends on the admitting diagnoses, and sadly, financial status. It could take four to six weeks to recover from a bout with pneumonia, but if insurance won't pay after a specific date and the resident doesn't have the funds to pay privately, the facility will often discharge the resident with a recommendation for an assisted living facility. It's the sad reality for some who cannot afford the services and exasperates their original problem of not having a safe environment to live in. The vicious cycle will continue.

There is a slight difference between the interchangeable terms "skilled nursing" and "nursing home" or "convalescent care." That difference is the length of stay and type of services offered. If your loved one is recovering, they will remain in the skilled nursing-rehabilitation section of the facility. When they reach a plateau in recovering their abilities, they may still need 24/7 convalescent care and will likely stay in the skilled nursing (non-rehabilitation) unit of the facility for long-term or permanent residency.

For Medicare coverage in a skilled facility, the resident has to be released from the hospital directly to skilled-rehab or convalescent care. There are many incidents of seniors being released to their home, and shortly after discovering they can't manage independently, they are informed that Medicare won't cover the cost of a skilled nursing home where they should have been sent in the first place. In your state, the hospitals may have policies regarding discharge from their care, and these policies can affect you financially. For example, in Washington state, a patient must be admitted, not under observation, for three qualifying midnights in order for Medicare to pick up part of the cost of a skilled rehab stay.

I recall an unfortunate occurrence when a resident had fallen ill and was sent to the hospital for evaluation. She had left mid-day on Monday and was admitted. This resident stayed in the hospital on Monday night and Tuesday night. She was released to a skilled nursing facility on Wednesday evening, just hours shy of the three-day qualifying hospital stay for Medicare to pay for her rehabilitation. In addition to the assisted living rent, she received a bill from the skilled-rehab facility after a six-week rehabilitation. As a result of the premature hospital discharge, the resident was responsible for the charges for the entire length of stay for rehabilitation, her assisted living rent, and the hospital bills. It was a major financial blow, and could have been prevented if she stayed in the hospital just a few hours longer to meet the requirements for Medicare coverage.

Each state varies with the coverage policies, and it's best to reach out to Medicare for specific information within your state to find out what the qualifying hospital stay is for skilled nursing coverage. If the requirements are not met, beneficiaries will be liable for substantial costs.

Chapter Two

HOW ASSISTED LIVING FACILITIES
FUNCTION

With mirth and laughter, let old wrinkles come.
—Merchant of Venice, William Shakespeare

S TAFFING WITHIN AN ASSISTED LIVING facility consists of department heads: the administrator, health services director, office manager, admissions coordinator, activities director, housekeeping director, maintenance director, and food services director. Depending on the size of the facility, there may be more or fewer positions, but these are the typical managers.

The department heads report to the administrator, who is in charge of operations within the facility. They ensure that all departments comply with the policies and procedures of the business as well as the state laws. The administrator manages the budget for the facility, reviews all incidents and documentation for all residents, assists with account collections, participates in marketing functions, remedies grievances, and much more. He or she is a busy person!

The health services director is the nurse for the building. Most of the time, they will be credentialed as either a registered nurse (RN) or licensed practical nurse (LPN).

The nurse manages the caregiving staff and provides direction to the resident care. He or she will write service plans and coordinate the daily tasks for each resident, and written instructions for the recommended services. All medical information passes through and is processed by the nurse. Some facilities will enlist the help of an assistant to handle the loads of paperwork involved in the admission process and assist with other tasks such as maintaining a schedule for the resident's showers, laundry and bed linens. The assistant and the nurse will oversee the staffing schedule for the caregivers and med-techs. The nurse bears an enormous responsibility, but this person does not replace the resident's doctor. In assisted living, the nurse is not authorized to diagnose a resident; they can communicate the symptoms and request prescription orders from the physician. This is done via fax, and the response time from the doctors vary. The nurse will ensure that the resident receives the appropriate care while awaiting further instruction from the doctor, and if it's urgent, the resident will be sent to the hospital for evaluation.

The maintenance and housekeeping directors work closely to keep the facility looking and smelling fresh. They generally maintain the carpets, common areas, and the resident apartments, as well as the facility grounds outside. The maintenance director will ensure that the building is up to code with fire safety and preventative maintenance.

The office manager is in charge of accounts payables, accounts receivables, payroll, and human resources. He or she juggles the tasks of crunching numbers while answering phones and greeting guests and therapists as they come in to visit the residents. The office manager will handle the billing of long-term care insurance and Medicaid claims.

The activities director facilitates the entertainment and exercise in the facility, promotes social interaction, and keeps the residents active and energized.

The food services director handles the kitchen operations, cooks the meals for the residents, purchases food and supplies, and maintains the kitchen to ensure it is up to code.

The admissions coordinator plays a key role in the successful operations of the facility. They are in charge of driving the census up. Most facilities are census driven, which means the staff hours are calculated by the number of residents, or population. If the facility is full and there are no vacancies, it can operate fully-staffed. If the building is down in census, staff hours must be reduced to accommodate the budget. Think of it as treading water; as long as the facility is fully occupied, it'll stay afloat. When there's a low census, the facility begins to sink. Quality goes down, consistency declines, and the care staff is run down both physically and emotionally as they must do twice the work in less time. If the admissions coordinator seems to press for a commitment, it's driven by the recognition of your loved one's need for assistance and the urgency to maintain the census. The admissions person markets the facility by visiting local hospitals, doctors' offices, clinics, and senior centers. They are actively involved in networking groups with fellow admissions coordinators and marketing professionals from neighboring facilities who work together to provide referrals and resources to those in need. The admissions coordinator you will meet should have a solid knowledge of the senior industry and compassion for the elderly. It takes a particular type of personality to work in this industry, given the challenges of time, budget, and pressure to keep the ball rolling with new prospects and continuous exposure to the facility.

Round the clock, hands-on attention to residents is provided by caregivers, identified as PCAs (personal care attendant) or CNAs (certified nursing assistant). A typical facility will have a med-tech, or person credentialed to dispense medications, and depending on the size of the facility, one caregiver for every ten to fifteen residents. Each facility is staffed differently, and some may have the ability to employ additional care staff.

In the years I've worked in an assisted living facility, the most common complaint from residents, family members, and the staff were that the facility is understaffed and the caregivers cannot keep up with the demands of the residents. From an insider's point of view, it is possible for the care staff to accommodate the residents' needs, and they work energetically to make it happen. It takes a strong team to communicate effectively and organize their tasks in an efficient way. An emergency may occur, diverting the care staff while other residents don't receive scheduled services such as removing garbage or making beds. The higher the acuity of care is within the facility, it becomes a challenge to accommodate someone requiring more intensive assistance, because it would distract caregivers from tending to other residents. During the initial assessment of a potential resident, the nurse reviews whether assisted living is appropriate or if the senior may need skilled nursing care.

Caregivers —the CNAs or PCAs—are frequently short-term employees. Many are students or just starting in the workforce and gathering experience before jumping to the next big thing. Other compassionate, kind, hard-working caregivers stay in the profession for many years. They aren't there just for the paycheck, but to enrich the lives of the residents. These employees will go above and beyond the call of duty to ensure the residents are happy and well cared for. You can pick these people out in a crowd; when you see a great caregiver, you'll know it.

Similarly, a harmonious team will be apparent. Their demeanor and positive attitude will be a reflection of great leadership from management.

When touring an assisted living facility, be sure to ask about the staff-to-resident ratio. Find out how the facility balances the staff to residents and maintains the quality of care. Ask if they have a nurse on-call after hours. Most of the health services directors will be on-call, as well as the administrator. Some facilities may have a designated nurse for this purpose. The key is to know that someone with authority and someone with nursing credentials will be available for emergencies after business hours.

Typically, assisted living facilities will not employ a house doctor to monitor the resident's health. Instead, the nurse communicates with the resident's primary care physician about medical changes or emergencies, requests that the resident call and set up an appointment to be seen by that physician, or sends them to the emergency room for an evaluation and further instruction.

Skilled nursing facilities commonly have a house doctor to oversee the resident's care and write discharge orders upon completion of their rehabilitation stay.

Some assisted living facilities use the outside services of a nurse practitioner who makes house calls to see residents who may have a difficult time getting to the doctor. The nurse practitioner has similar authority as a primary physician and can write orders for medication and therapies. If the facility you're touring has access to a doctor or nurse practitioner, it can take some of the stress away, saving you from having to take time off work for doctor visits.

MONEY, MONEY, MONEY

Before we proceed, let's discuss the burning question: how much does assisted living cost?

It's the one question I found the most challenging to answer, because the cost varies from person to person. The price is determined by how much or how little assistance the potential resident will require.

All facilities differ with their pricing, and demographics usually influence the price ranges. To give a clear understanding of how pricing is set, I'll use a general example.

Upon move-in, your loved one can expect to pay a one-time fee up front, referred to as a move-in fee or community fee. This charge will cover the cost of damages such as scuffed walls and doors, heavy odors, holes, and carpets. The facility's cost to maintain the apartments and keep them fresh is quite high, and the fee helps to keep the building well maintained.

The facility will charge a monthly rental fee, which is in the thousands. No matter which state you live in, a facility charges an average base rent of anywhere between $2,000 to $7,000 per month. These prices have nearly doubled in the past decade and typically increase annually. When projecting how much money your loved one has, and how long they can make it last within a particular facility, be sure to take into consideration a modest price increase of about three percent each year.

In addition to the monthly rental fee, the facility may charge a level of care (LOC) or an ala carte for activities of daily living (ADL) services. This could be several hundred dollars added to the base rent. Again, this is facility and state-specific, but my examples will give you a rough idea so you will know what to expect when shopping around.

The level of care is determined by the nurse, and the services are usually bundled into a LOC package. The frequency of the assistance, type of assistance, and preference will be a factor in raising or decreasing the LOC that is assessed. For example, if your loved one doesn't require much help and needs reminders and queuing, they would be on the lower end of the LOC 1 or LOC 2 price. If they need hands-on assistance or if they require complex medication management, they'll be on the higher end of a LOC 3 or LOC 4 price range.

Ala carte services are just that. You can select each service and pay for them as needed. Does your loved one's dog need to be taken on walks by the caregivers? That's going to cost you each time. The benefit is the freedom to choose what your loved one needs vs. being bundled into a set price. The benefits to LOC charges are the opposite. While one option may be excellent for someone, the latter could be preferable to another.

The range of pricing is so vast between each facility in each state and per person, that it's impossible to predict exactly how much assisted living costs, but these examples will give you a good place to start.

Bear in mind the basic elements of the cost and know that the needs of the resident drive the price.

MEDICAID

Medicare, the federal health insurance program for people age 65 and over, does not cover assisted living expenses. Even coverage of skilled nursing care facilities is limited. Medicaid is the joint federal/state program that covers medical costs for some people with limited income and resources, but Medicaid enrollment can be complicated.

Depending on the state you live in, Medicaid may be referred to by an alternative name (such as Apple Health in Washington state), but the processes are similar. I suggest you contact your state's long-term care agency to verify any information. Programs change often and aren't the same in every state.

As an example, here's how things work in Washington state: let's say Margaret has exhausted her savings. She no longer has any assets, and she's living off of her Social Security income. Her primary care physician diagnoses her with a medically necessary requirement for assisted living, and she meets the state guidelines for the diagnoses.

Margaret will need to complete and submit an application for service initiation to The Department of State Health Services, or DSHS. These applications can be obtained by calling the local DSHS office or visiting the DSHS website. Once the application is submitted, she will be assigned a caseworker, and an assessment is scheduled. This assessment will consist of the caseworker reviewing Margaret's medical history, gathering demographic information, and verifying her medically necessary needs.

While awaiting the assessment, Margaret will gather all of her financial documentation from the last five years (this varies per state, also) to include bank statements and proof to track where all of her money had been spent. Essentially, she will be required to validate that she didn't "give it all away" to a friend or family, or invested it somewhere, or cashed out a lump sum of money.

Upon completion of the assessment, the case is transferred to a DSHS financial caseworker. From there, the financial caseworker will review everything thoroughly and request additional documents if there are financial questions.

Assuming that all financial requirements are met per state regulations, and the medical assessment has been approved and processed, Margaret will receive a confirmation of approval for long-term care services from DSHS with an effective date. Depending on the state, the letter will also include a monthly amount owed to the assisted living facility, which is usually the Social Security monthly payment less a meager amount for personal expenses. In Washington state, Margaret is able to retain about $60 per month. The monthly amount can fluctuate if she has medical expenses that are not covered by Medicaid; she would submit a receipt for those expenses to her caseworker, who then adjusts the amount owed for that particular month to offset the cost.

Now that you know the enrollment process (once more, it varies from state to state, so this example is generic but closely resembles the process), here's how Medicaid works in the assisted living environment and why it is difficult to find a facility that has immediate openings for a Medicaid resident.

As I mentioned above, a facility charges an average of $2,000 to $7,000 for private pay residents. In Washington state, Medicaid pays a maximum of around $1,800 per month. Also, the state requires the assisted living facility to furnish all toiletries and personal hygiene items such as toilet paper, tissue, shampoo, and more. Other miscellaneous charges such as late fees or room service fees cannot be charged to the resident; therefore, the facility must provide some services free of charge. The assisted living facility loses a significant amount of money to house a senior on Medicaid when the Medicaid payment barely covers the cost of food or wages.

"You don't have any openings? What are we supposed to do? This is outrageous!" says the distressed family member on the phone. Outrageous? Absolutely. From a family member's standpoint, it's terrifying to run into this obstacle. It is not necessarily the facility's fault but the responsibility of state lawmakers who set the Medicaid reimbursement rates. To put it into perspective, a senior on Medicaid in an assisted living facility has access to medical professionals, physical and occupational therapist services, meals, housekeeping, maintenance, social activities, hygiene products, amenities and personal services typically not provided at home, for a price that is comparable to a non-assisted apartment in town. The facility will budget for a particular number of apartments to house Medicaid paying residents, but they must accommodate those who are currently in the facility and "spending down" their savings. Once all of the current resident's funds are exhausted, they, too, will begin the Medicaid enrollment process. The facility will likely continue their residency if the resident has met a two or three-year private pay requirement before accepting Medicaid.

NO MEDICAID OPENINGS? NOW WHAT?

Let's say your loved one receives a letter and is approved for Medicaid benefits. You pick up the phone and begin calling a few of the local assisted living facilities to inquire about their availability. Each community tells you that they don't have any Medicaid openings at this time and their waitlist is one year long. You hang up, feeling defeated, angry and lost.

Now what?

You're in a situation that many others are experiencing, and it's going to take resilience to overcome this challenge.

Fortunately, there are a few temporary solutions while we wait for an opening. Each circumstance will be different, and these solutions may not be appropriate for everyone, but it will give you a good place to start.

Assuming you're not in crisis-mode and considering your loved one is living independently; the first step would be to secure their environment. Remove obstacles and hazards that may cause a fall, replace unsafe furniture (anything with wheels, low to the ground, plush couches or chairs), check the refrigerator for spoiled food, and look for expired medications.

Next, set up an appointment with the primary care physician and bring your loved one to frequent checkups to ensure that medication doses are accurate, and to keep track of her health.

If it's affordable, furnish an emergency call-button that she can wear or has easy access to in case of emergency. Your loved one may not always be near a phone, and if something happens, she can call for help right away. Some of these emergency call-button services require a contract, so find out if those contracts can be canceled once she moves into an assisted living facility.

Home care agencies are a terrific resource if something comes up and you're unable to assist your loved one. It's possible that some services will be covered by Medicaid, but most likely will be an out-of-pocket expense.

Medications can be set up weekly in a pill organizer, and if you have the ability, set reminders or alerts to notify your loved one when it's time to take their meds. Take advantage of the automatic pill dispensers that feature a timer and lock, for those with memory impairments.

In the meantime, you'll want to stay in contact with the admissions coordinators in the facilities who put you on their wait-list. When an apartment becomes available, they will let you know, but this could be a lengthy wait. The wait-list status is unpredictable and can change in a matter of days or months. It's all a budget-balancing act within the facility. Believe me; it's heart-wrenching to be on the other end of the phone, continually bearing the bad news to seniors in need of help.

Another option while you wait is to move your loved one into your own home. Many family members try this route and take turns assisting with daily care, although this option is not the best for either party. Perhaps your home is accessible for someone with limited mobility and you're comfortable providing care, but the truth is, they're going to miss out on the social activities, therapy services, and professional medical services. If you've run out of time and needed to make a move immediately, this may be a short-term remedy.

Finally, an adult family home is a possible location for your loved one to reside while awaiting a Medicaid opening in an assisted living facility. An adult family home is a private residential setting for those with complex health needs such as chronic illnesses, specific disabilities, or advanced stages of dementia. This option might be unavailable for most, but I recommend researching the requirements for residency and see if it applies to your situation.

Reach out to the senior resources in your area and maintain perseverance. The more live wires you have out there, the better chance you'll have at getting the next available Medicaid opening. It may seem like all hope is lost, but remain persistent and be ready at all times.

Chapter Three

BEGINNING THE SEARCH

By failing to prepare, you are preparing to fail.
—Benjamin Franklin

*A*FTER RECOGNIZING THAT YOUR loved one needs help or if directed by a physician, it's time to begin your search for an assisted living facility. There are a few things to consider before you pick up the phone.

Understandably, the location of the facility is important to a family member, as they will want their loved one to be nearby. There may be several siblings living across numerous states, but the general location of the assisted living should be selected at the discretion of your loved one. It may be inconvenient for family to travel, but ultimately the decision should come from the person who will be living there.

Furthermore, moving a medically compromised senior across the states could be risky and has been known to cause a rapid decline in cognitive functions as they adjust to their new home.

If applicable, the person with power of attorney who makes medical and financial decisions should have easy access to the resident. Most assisted living facilities recommend that the resident's family advocate be present for medical conferences and that they're available for emergencies, especially if the resident is transferred to the hospital. Additionally, the facility will reach out and request that you stop by when your loved one is feeling anxious or expressing negative behaviors, and the staff is unsuccessful with redirecting them.

In addition to location, it's essential to identify what will be more comfortable for your loved one. Is a smaller, more intimate facility more desirable than the large, fifteen-story building? Would they prefer a home-like-setting or a resort-setting? Luxury or down-home? Are they active and would enjoy going for a dip in the pool? Perhaps they would be most comfortable in a facility that includes church services on the weekend and a theater that plays new-release movies.

Whatever their primary desire may be, create a list for them and ensure that you ask about those services or amenities.

A Google search online for "assisted living" accompanied with the location of your loved one's preference will provide a list of facilities in that vicinity and public reviews. I urge you to read through the online reviews but with caution. Online reviews are posted when something wonderful happens and someone is grateful, or when something terrible happens and someone is angry. There will always be that one person who cannot be pleased, or they were dissatisfied with the resolution. Some reviews sound downright awful, and it makes you wonder what happened. Take note of how the assisted living facility responds to the reviews, and it will offer useful insight to see what types of problems occur within and how they are received by management.

Reviews are to be taken with a grain of salt, as we do not know the context in which the issue had arisen. They serve a purpose for exposing the facility's reputation; you'd be more inclined to call the facility with a higher reputation and several five-star reviews over another facility with a handful of two-star reviews.

Internet searches are the most accessible tool, but there are other resources for your search. Stop into a grocery store and pick up a senior living magazine near the free newspapers and advertisements. You can also stop by local hospitals and request information.

INITIAL PHONE CALLS

When you are ready to call and request information, you'll want to speak with the admissions coordinator. Their role is to answer questions about the facility, gather basic information about your loved one and the current living environment, and to schedule tours. Tours are available at any time, but it's best to schedule it for a time when the admissions coordinator is present. Some larger facilities will have more than one admissions coordinator to cover weekends.

If you scheduled a tour with someone and you're not able to make it to the appointment, please remember to call and reschedule. The staff is understanding, but it can be discouraging for the admissions coordinator to come in on their day off and their tour appointment is a no-show. I speak from experience. I recall a Saturday morning when I missed my son's football game because I had scheduled a weekend tour with a prospective resident. I waited in my office and called this client after the scheduled time came and went, but he didn't answer my call or show up to his appointment. It was rather unfortunate and I don't know what his circumstances were, but I hope to convey some encouragement to send a text or make a quick call if you need more time.

There are several questions to ask upfront. What is the current availability for an apartment? The facility may have a waiting list that may be several weeks to several months long and might not meet your timeline.

Do they accept Medicaid? Check to make sure that the facility is currently contracted with Medicaid. There may be some facilities which are not participating in the program, or worse, have had their Medicaid license revoked. You will likely hear about the minimum private pay requirement policy, if any, and their current Medicaid wait-list status.

Do they accept long-term care insurance policies? If you have one, be sure to find out if the facility has the ability to submit claims for processing. Some long-term care insurance policies have clauses that could eliminate your loved one's eligibility for reimbursement. For example, the policy may state that the resident is to receive "nursing services" within the facility, however, assisted living facilities are not authorized to provide nursing services. They are, instead, classified as "custodial" services. Some policies are very old, and contain verbiage that is outdated and does not apply. These types of loopholes could be costly, if not discovered ahead of time.

Do they allow pets? In pet-friendly facilities, there is usually a pet fee and weight limit. Consider if the pet could be a trip hazard or if your loved one can care for the pet independently to determine if it's truly necessary. Sometimes, it's a deal-breaker if pets are not allowed, but remember to think about the long-term.

Ask about services and amenities on the list that you have made, and keep track of the facilities which include the desired features, and the facilities who have other comparable features.

Decide on a convenient time to book a tour and create a manageable list for your schedule that day. If your loved one who is cognitively or physically unable to the perform the task, consider touring the facilities without them and eliminating those facilities which you feel would not be appropriate for their preferences and needs. Taking the first step can cause anxiety and trigger some powerful emotions for your loved one, all of which can be avoided by checking things out first and deciding on the top three facilities to re-tour. Then bring them along. This is a time for you to build a professional relationship with the admissions coordinator. A successful transition relies heavily on trust between both parties so that the assisted living can take your word when you tell them about your loved one's behaviors and routines, and you will trust that the facility will take excellent care of your loved one. All of the details are important when discussing your loved one's current situation.

Chapter Four

THE TOURS

Every day is a journey, and the journey itself is home.
—Matsuo Basho

WHEN YOU ARRIVE FOR YOUR tour, there are some things to pay close attention to. First impressions are paramount. It's an indication as to how the staff treats guests and residents. Some of these suggestions may seem obvious, but I am highlighting a few particular observations to be mindful of, because unaddressed issues can be the cause of much deeper-rooted problems within the assisted living facility.

You may be feeling a bit overwhelmed and anxious, and the last thing on your mind is paying attention to the small details. This is completely normal, so don't let these feelings intimidate you. Be confident that you are going in prepared and that your purpose is to find a safe environment for your loved one. If you don't understand something, ask. If the answer is still unclear, ask again, no matter how trivial it may seem. The admissions coordinator will follow up with you after the tour to see if you had any other questions that may have come up.

The first impression happens as soon as you enter the parking lot. Are the grounds maintained? Are the walking paths cleared? Does it feel warm and inviting, or cold and institutional? What about the view from the apartments? Will your loved one be looking out at a lush, green courtyard with lots of trees and gardens? Or at an abandoned building littered with trash and graffiti?

Next, enter the building and take a deep breath. Does it smell like cats and mothballs? Neutral and odorless? Or freshly baked cookies? The facility should maintain their carpets, hallways, and apartments to prevent offensive odors from permeating the common areas. In some states, it is against regulations to use deodorizers and air fresheners, as they consider this a "cover-up." Be advised that there are occasional incontinent accidents that occur within the building, and the aftermath lingers temporarily after the caregivers have assisted and remedied the situation. I've had to explain this to many guests during a tour when exiting the elevator, and I noticed their eyes watering or nose wrinkling. Unfortunately, odors like this leave a wrong impression when guests don't know the source. Try to use your better judgment and determine if it's due to lack of maintenance or merely an accident. On the other hand, if pleasant scents of fresh bread or chocolate chip cookies wafts your way, it's a good sign. It means that the residents are in the activity room socializing, and hopefully, there will be plenty of treats to share!

Take note of the residents' condition. Are the men clean shaven? Do the ladies have their hair done? Are their clothes neat and tidy, or covered with food stains? Observing the residents for their appearance will provide an example of how attentive the staff will be with your loved one. If the residents appear to be appropriately groomed, this is an indication that the caregiving staff spent their time well and thoroughly prepared the resident for the day. If the residents appear to be in need of hygiene attention, this can indicate that the staff rushed the resident through their morning routine and skipped a few steps.

Next, are staff members friendly and helpful? Are they smiling and visiting with the residents as they walk by? Observe their demeanor for positive traits, and this will indicate that the staff members are happy to be there.

If all checks out and the building doesn't have an odor, the residents appear to be happy and healthy, and the staff is observed to be friendly, you're ready to begin the tour.

THE TOUR – DISCOVERY

When the admissions coordinator meets with you, you'll have the chance to talk face-to-face about what you're looking for within the facility, and discuss the needs of your loved one. The facilities call this part of the tour "discovery" because they will listen to everything you have to say, and conclude if assisted living would be suitable for your loved one. Start by explaining the purpose of your visit, and tell them about your loved one's current situation. It's important to disclose any unusual or difficult behaviors that your loved one displays, as this will be part of the determination process for the coordinator to know if your loved one will be an appropriate fit for the facility.

Also, be sure to talk about their medical diagnosis as best as you can. Certain conditions require care beyond the assisted living level, and a nurse must explicitly manage those conditions.

Financial status should be disclosed, whether your loved one will be paying privately or if they will be running out of funds within the near future and require Medicaid to cover the cost.

It is challenging to know what the exact monthly rate would be for your loved one at that point in the tour because the nurse will need to complete an assessment and review your loved one's medical history. The admissions coordinator can give you a ballpark estimate based on the information you give to them. You can decide whether or not it will fit within your loved one's budget and proceed from there.

THE TOUR – WITHIN THE FACILITY

You've discussed your loved one's situation, and you're ready to see what the facility has to offer. The admissions coordinator will begin the tour, and generally, lead with historical facts about the company. Listen as they talk about their core values and what is most important to their success. Core values rooted in providing excellent care to the resident supersede luxurious amenities and features. You're going to want to choose a facility that employs staff with kind hearts and integrity. They will create the compassionate culture within.

You will likely meet the department head team. Each will talk a bit about their department and what they have to offer. This is your opportunity to ask specific questions about the department and get answers straight from the source.

As you go along the tour, take notes or record conversations on your phone. All of this information can be overwhelming at first. There are so many details that you'll want to review before making the decision. It's helpful to have your list of questions ready and stay organized with the literature and brochures that are given to you.

Those who take a tour and remain silent, allowing for the admissions coordinator to do all of the speaking, are less successful in placing their loved ones as opposed to those who are actively a part of the tour and communicating what their needs are. Admissions coordinators are trained to listen; they cannot help you until you tell them what you need. It is essential to be as transparent as possible. There will be some cases in which your loved one's needs may exceed the services of assisted living and will require skilled nursing care. It's best to discover this before placing your loved one in an environment that won't be appropriate. It will seem like there are many questions, some extremely personal, but it is a part of the discovery and transition process.

Trust your gut as you go along for the tour. If you are sensing something that doesn't feel right, if the staff doesn't make you feel welcome, or if the facility doesn't appeal to you, you should consider other options. I'm sure we have all experienced this feeling that either brings uncertainty or apprehension. If it's caused by the people who will be entrusted with your loved one's care, you may be right. Keep an open mind, and genuinely study the behavior to make sure it's not just your nerves or emotions getting in the way. This decision is an important one, and it's up to you to make the right one. No pressure, right?

THE TOUR – ROOMS & APARTMENTS

You'll most likely tour the most desirable apartment or room that is currently available. Most facilities will have studio apartments, one bedroom, two bedrooms, and even three-bedroom apartments. They vary in size and layout, but they will all feature barrier-free accommodations.

If you enter a studio apartment, the first thing you might think is, wow, this is small. Studio apartments will have a kitchenette, bathroom, and small living space with an alcove or designated area for a bed. They are very basic, and if your loved one is moving from a large home, this option would seem nearly impossible to downsize. Studio apartments would be ideal for those who are less mobile, or more advanced in stages of dementia and will spend most of their time in the common areas. The benefit of a studio apartment is the cost. For some, a smaller space can be comforting.

A one-bedroom apartment is a little larger, and the fundamental difference between a studio and a one bedroom (in the average facility) is a wall that separates the bedroom from the rest of the apartment. The cost is a few hundred dollars difference. However, the extra room and added wall space could be a necessary feature to someone. One-bedroom apartments are the most popular. If there are none available, the resident could move into a studio and transfer to a one-bedroom when it becomes available.

The two-bedroom apartments are ideal for a couple who require extensive medical care or sleep in separate beds or have a different sleep schedule. This size apartment is also convenient for those with family who comes from out of town and needs a place to stay when visiting. Of course, the larger the apartment, the more personal belongings will fit. It's a difficult thing, downsizing, but keep in mind the safety factor and potential trip hazards with too much "stuff."

The standard kitchenette within an assisted living apartment will include a small sink, counter, cupboards, drawers, microwave and refrigerator/freezer. The kitchenette allows the resident to make a snack and store leftover foods, but food cannot be cooked in the apartment since most do not furnish a stove or oven. As the resident's cognitive ability declines, so does safety awareness. Removing potentially hazardous items such as kitchen appliances prevents an accidental burning or cutting on sharp objects as well as reduces the risk of unsafe food handling, preparation, and consumption. Instead, the facility has a full-size commercial kitchen and dietary staff to prepare all meals and snacks for the residents. Depending on the location, there may be an additional kitchen in the common area such as an activity room for the residents to use at their leisure.

Take into account the condition of the apartment. In older facilities, apartments may seem a bit outdated, but the maintenance staff should at least maintain the flooring, walls, and appliances.

Carpeting should not be plush with a thick pad underneath, as this can create unsteady footing. Some facilities will not use a pad at all to heighten the stability of the resident's furniture and for easy mobility with a walker or wheelchair. Low-pile carpets are ideal in a facility and are much easier to maintain. Long fibers and shaggy rugs are difficult to keep clean and become flattened and tattered with constant traffic from a wheelchair or walker. Laminate floors may look pretty, but they can be the most dangerous. A slip from a dry sock or drop of water and a consequent fall could lead to broken bones.

Place your loved one's furniture with your mind, and imagine where you can put the items that are most valuable to them. Can you visualize where you could put the couch or recliner? How about the TV and bookshelf? Maybe there is enough wall space to bring their favorite tapestry and pictures of the grandchildren, right next to the portrait of their wedding day. Remember to be practical and bring only what they will need. You may have to put the rest in a storage facility or discuss among the family and your loved one what they wish to do with the items that will not be coming.

If the apartment features a patio or balcony, evaluate if this would be beneficial to your loved one, or a risk. Those who have shown exit-seeking behaviors may not be safe renting a ground floor apartment with a patio enabling them to wander off and get lost.

Finally, the bathrooms should be large enough to navigate a walker or wheelchair, and the showers should be barrier-free. Standard facilities will have walk-in showers without bathtubs to step over. If they don't already have grab bars installed, the facility should offer permission to have them installed for added safety. The resident can purchase a shower chair or bench and use it for safe showering.

Could you imagine your loved one living here? Look out the windows and take into account the surrounding area. Will they enjoy the serene courtyard? Or maybe they would prefer to watch the hustle and bustle of a busy parking lot or street? Do you feel comfortable? Is it quiet and peaceful? Some facilities are very busy and tend to get a little noisy with music and entertainment, but this tactic encourages socialization among the residents. Is it a long way from the facility dining room? If your loved one has mobility limitations, consider the benefits or hindrances to the apartment location.

Most importantly, when deciding on your top three facilities, do consider what your loved one would prefer above your own preferences. After all, they will be the one to call it home.

THE TOUR – HOUSEKEEPING SERVICES

Housekeeping services are standard in most assisted living facilities. As we age, maintaining a living space becomes more demanding. For some, it may become a physical challenge.

Some of the services that are common and may be included are vacuuming, light dusting, kitchenette and bathroom cleaning, and garbage removal. This is generally done once a week. However, if the resident requires additional services above the standard for an incontinence issue, or perhaps a desire for extra garbage removal, the facility will add supplementary housekeeping services to the resident's service plan for a fee. Extra service means the level of care increases.

Assisted living facilities perform a background check on staff members who are in direct contact with the residents, and this includes housekeeping staff. Background check requirements vary from state to state. The housekeepers I've known and worked with are honest and ethical individuals. They are hired with the knowledge that they will be in residents' apartments, among their valuables. The facility will ensure that they find someone who can be trusted around vulnerable adults. That said, we all know there can be bad apples in the basket, and desperate people have been known to do desperate things. Avoid bringing something of value into the apartment to prevent the heartache of having it lost or stolen. Even though these things don't happen often, we must remain vigilant to protect our loved ones and their valuables.

Be prepared: there are reports of missing items all the time. Theft is not always the cause of their disappearance. Ninety percent of missing items are located within the resident's apartment as a result of confusion, dementia or forgetfulness. The residents with dementia will not know that they left their purse in the refrigerator or their keys in the empty coffee mug. They tend to assume that the housekeeper or a staff member had moved or taken the item. Small things such as towels and laundry turn up missing often, but after a search by the care staff or housekeeper, the items are sometimes found in another resident's apartment from a result of getting mixed up in the laundry room. Where I once worked, a housekeeper, Roxy, could find missing items better than a bloodhound. She knew the residents' behaviors and schedules and could predict which apartment could be holding the missing things. She would spend time visiting with the residents while cleaning their apartments and recognize if something wasn't quite right, and she would report her observations to the nurse. Sometimes, heroes don't wear capes. They drag vacuums.

It is not uncommon for other residents to take belongings and bring them back into their apartment, thinking it belongs to them. Facility items are often located within the apartments: cups, napkins, plates, cutlery, and even cupboards full of sugar packets and tea bags. The residents who do this are not maliciously intending to steal. They're just pleasantly confused. Many residents grew up during the Depression and revert to the salvage and reuse mindset. It's an easy behavior to handle, and although it most likely cannot be reversed, the housekeeping and care staff will collect the items that do not belong to the resident and return them to their owners.

THE TOUR – TRANSPORTATION

Inquire about the facility's transportation services, and if it's complimentary, or offered for a fee. Most facilities will have a designated bus or van with a wheelchair lift to transport residents to and from the doctor's office, as well as planned activity outings. There may be designated days in which the bus provides transportation, and if so, remember to schedule future appointments on those particular days. Often, facility transportation will not go past a ten-mile-radius from the building, because longer trips can cause lengthy delays in picking up or dropping off the next person for their appointment.

How do they do it when one person has an appointment at 9:00 a.m., and two other residents could have an appointment at 9:15 a.m. clear across town? The facility will juggle these appointments by arranging the drop-offs according to the locations, and sometimes the resident will need to need to arrive fairly early and wait. If this will be an issue for your loved one, then you may want to stick to being their sole method of transportation to avoid having to make them wait. Most residents do not mind waiting and are content to sit in the lobby with a magazine and hot cup of coffee. However, there are others who are a bit more advanced with memory impairments, and become anxious while waiting. If this is the case, you can check with the facility and see about sending a caregiver to ride along with your loved one, just in case you get in a pinch and can't make it to the appointment. Chances are, the facility will provide this service only if their staffing situation allows for it, and they will usually charge an additional fee.

THE TOUR – SOCIAL ACTIVITIES

Social activities are not only fun for seniors, but also beneficial. Your loved one might be reclusive or seemingly not interested in participating in any activity in a facility room or chatting with other residents. They might be the type of person who is content to stay in their apartment and watch old Westerns all day long.

A successful activity director is bold, assertive, enthusiastic and maybe even a little wild. He or she is the type of person willing to dress up in crazy hats just for fun and dances down the hallway to gather residents for the next activity. It takes a confident individual to bring sunshine into the residents' lives each day.

During your tour, pick up an activity calendar. Typically, you may see exercise listed on the schedule at least a few times a week. As the adage goes, "Use it, or lose it." It's especially true with the senior population; if they do not exercise regularly, they will lose their strength and balance.

Often seniors do not like to exercise. They will find any reason not to do it and refuse the invitation to participate. A conscientious activity director will continue to re-approach until they can roust the residents out of their chairs and into the activity room.

The power of suggestion is huge. Assisted living facilities are legally not authorized to tell a resident what to do; rather, the staff can only suggest and encourage. As you may assume, this is challenging with the senior population, and as a result, the staff must discover alternative methods to encourage the residents to perform routine tasks such as taking a shower, eating their meal instead of just the desserts, and participating in activities. If your loved one isn't keen on socializing, let the staff know and see what they can do to turn it around. You'll be quite surprised to find out that a lot of the residents who moved in went from little-to-no participation, to calling out the bingo numbers and planting the facility garden in a matter of months.

At my former assisted living facility where I worked, I was very fond of an activity director, Shari, who had a gift for successfully encouraging the residents to participate in her activities. She would arrive to work early, while the residents were eating breakfast in the dining room. Shari would walk from table to table and announce the activities for that day.

She generated hype and a buzz of excitement among the residents. By the time her activities began, the activity room was full of residents, eager to socialize and have fun. All it took was creative prompting from a delightful activity director.

Exercise programs vary in each facility. Some may include walks around the courtyard or the local mall. They may consist of balloon volleyball within a small circle, or a Tai Chi class. Each resident will have a different level of ability for participating in the class, and those who are unable to walk can still join and have fun. The first step is getting the resident to the activity room. Once the activity director succeeds in breaking the ice and showing the resident that everyone can do it no matter what physical barriers they have, we start to see progress toward maintaining an active, healthy lifestyle.

Find out if the activities are personalized or tracked. This means that the residents who are reluctant to participate are getting additional help, and the activity director is tracking reasons why residents aren't actively involved. Sometimes, a resident just needs a shoulder to cry on, or someone to listen to their grievances. Other situations may be that a resident is embarrassed to participate because he or she is incontinent and doesn't want anyone to notice. Everyone is different, and the activity director will find a way to encourage them to come out of their apartment and show them how much fun it is to play.

The game of bingo is highly anticipated and popular in the senior community. I've seen some bingo sessions last over four hours! The significant part about this game is that it uses cognitive skills to search for a letter and corresponding number across a board, and it isn't physically demanding. People of all ages have loved this game for its competitive nature and the thrill of calling out "BINGO!" While this is not a requirement for an assisted living facility activity, it is a plus indeed.

If the facility cannot offer such games, find out what the alternative plan is to provide entertainment to the residents. Do they take the residents to the local senior center? Do they offer volunteer opportunities? Do they go offsite to places such as the casino or the park? If so, does the staff offer assistance to those who will require extra help getting around? You will find that activities are just as important as personal care, because it truly enriches residents' daily lives by stimulating their minds and bodies.

THE TOUR – PET CARE

As mentioned earlier, before committing to bringing an animal to the assisted living apartment, ask yourself: is it a good idea for your loved one to care for a pet at this time?

Pets are great for companionship, but they can also become a safety hazard and a burden. It's understandable how challenging it can be to convince someone to give up a pet or choose just one of many to bring along.

If your loved one cannot maintain an animal in their apartment, this might be a good time for you or a family member to adopt their pet and provide care for it. It may not be possible because of your own situation, but perhaps a friend would be interested in adoption.

As a last resort, if all other options are exhausted, reach out to the local animal shelter or place an ad on Craigslist to find a new home for the pet. Ensure that your loved one is involved with this process, and never make any decision unless they agree. Pets are like people to some; placing them up for adoption can be traumatic and emotional. Be cautious and tread lightly to avoid creating stress.

On the opposite end of the spectrum, owning a pet in an assisted living facility can be delightful! If your loved one is capable of providing care for a pet, then I encourage you to assist with the transition and acclimating it to the new facility. Keeping a pet will promote exercise when a dog needs to go outside for a walk, and it is a social attribute to bring cheer to the other residents. Many folks love animals, and it brightens their day when they have the opportunity to love on a pet. Be mindful that some residents may not like particular animals, so be sure that the pet is well behaved and on a leash at all times.

Pets must be vaccinated and maintained to comply with state regulations. During your conversation with the admissions coordinator, determine which pet-documents you'll need to bring prior to move-in.

THE TOUR – FOOD SERVICES

In assisted living, mealtimes are a significant part of a senior's day. Facilities will serve breakfast, lunch, and dinner, and offer snacks to the residents who are out and about, missed a meal, or for those who have diabetes and require a little boost to adjust their insulin levels.

As we age, we lose part of our sense of taste due to the number of our taste buds declining and shrinking. Medications, diseases, and other factors can compound this decline, and many will lose the ability to distinguish between sweet and salty, bitter and sour. It is common in an assisted living facility to hear from some residents about how terrible the food is, while others claim it is the best they've ever had. Many complain about the food; however, it is usually unrelated to how the food actually tastes. Often, the resident could be having a troublesome day, or may be in a fair amount of pain and thus difficult to please. There are days when nothing can make them smile, no matter what lengths the staff goes to perk them up. Complaining about the food is an outlet for the resident, because their tablemates will sometimes agree and sympathize, and the staff will provide extra attention to the resident in an attempt to bring them something they'll enjoy.

Generally speaking, the food prepared in an assisted living facility comes from a food supplier who delivers the frozen products to the kitchen, and much of this is pre-packaged and pre-cooked. Commonly, the food is prepared as oven-baked and served with preserved items.

There is a "no salt" added regulation, as high levels of sodium could cause medical emergencies or conflict with certain medications. Meals tend to be somewhat bland, however salt and pepper are available for residents to season their food according to their preference at their table or in their apartment. For those with a keen sense of taste, this might be slightly disappointing to know that the food is not quite restaurant quality, and this is due to a state regulation that the facilities are obligated to follow. It is a challenge for the chefs to prepare a meal up to their high standards based on their own taste preference, but the staff must adhere to the rules.

Many facilities boast that they have gourmet, chef-prepared meals. While this may be true, the fact remains that the state regulates how that food is prepared. This is different from a restaurant. The ingredients and balance of proteins, grains, and more must meet the regulations for the facility to be in compliance. For example, the chef cannot purchase ingredients from a fresh farmer's market, or use fresh vegetables grown in the facility's garden. They must be purchased from a retail supplier who can provide information about where the product originated and certification that the food was handled safely, and is unadulterated.

Not everyone will be pleased, as the state regulations prevent the facility from serving many favorite food items, but we should respect that we have these regulations for a good reason. Safety is always paramount.

I recall an instance when Patricia, a resident's family member, submitted a formal complaint to Chelsey, the manager at the time. Patricia felt that the facility did not provide enough fresh fruit during mealtimes. She insisted that the weather was hot, and the fruits are on sale and plentiful, so she expected the facility to purchase and serve fresh, locally grown fruit. When Chelsey explained to her that the regulations mandate that they cannot serve anything that hasn't been purchased from a retail supplier, Patricia was upset and dissatisfied. Chelsey apologized profusely and said that Patricia was more than welcome to buy her own fresh fruits for her mother, and she could consume them in the comfort of her apartment or at her dining room table, but the facility was unable to accommodate the request to provide locally grown fruit during mealtimes. Once again, Patricia was upset, but Chelsey could only adhere to the regulations. This is a prime example of what happens when a family member did not understand or agree with the regulations and blamed the facility for their dissatisfaction. Do try to be understanding and reasonable when sharing your opinion and preference. Some things simply cannot be accommodated. On the other hand, if your request is within reason, I encourage you to visit with the food services director and let them know if there's something special you'd like to see on the menu.

Most facilities have predetermined menus, at least a few days to a week out. The staff orders enough products to prepare the meals, and in the event of a food recall or missing ingredient, the staff will have ample time to prepare an alternative meal. Some facilities will welcome requests and work them into the menu, as long as they can maintain the recommended daily nutrition levels as approved by a dietician.

During a meal, your loved one can expect a few different things depending on the facility. If the facility offers restaurant-style dining, she will sit at a table with other residents who share similar interests or personality. Typically, that table will become her designated seat during mealtimes, but there are no assigned seats. Your loved one will be waited on by a staff member and given meal entre choices balanced with soup or salad, and dessert.

If a facility offers buffet-style dining, your loved one will prepare a plate with items of his choosing from a buffet line. It is much easier for some seniors to receive the service at their tables, due to the mobility issues that can get a little more difficult with walkers, wheelchairs, motorized scooters and more. Buffet-style dining is appropriate for someone who is independent and can carry their plate safely without the risk of falling or stumbling.

When a resident is ill or recovering from a recent injury, the caregivers will deliver meals to the resident's room. Some facilities may charge a fee for this service, so be sure to ask when touring. The residents are encouraged to remain in their apartment when they are sick to prevent the spread of illness to others with compromised immune systems. There should be no charge for delivering meals to the apartments for those who cannot come out of their room during recovery. Charges are implemented when room trays or room service becomes habitual, and the resident no longer receives the brief social and exercise exposure. The delivery fee is to discourage the residents from avoiding coming out of their apartment to the dining room for meals. It is easy for a resident to slip into this comfort zone, and they will begin removing themselves from the activity and interaction of the other residents. Soon, they will decline rapidly and become content to stay in bed all day. Of course, this is not good for obvious reasons; loss of muscle, hygiene issues, depression, and more. The staff will notify the family if they sense a pattern of room trays, and a family intervention usually resolves the situation.

Many facilities will monitor the resident's weight for gains or losses, and notify the physician accordingly. If the resident has lost a fair amount of weight, the nurse will check the records to see if he or she has been attending the meals, and the nurse will request that the care staff document how much that resident had eaten. After monitoring for a short time, the nurse can determine if the weight loss is due to a lack of caloric intake, or if there is a medical reason. Either way, the resident's primary physician will be notified, and the nurse will await further instructions. If the physician deems it necessary to see the resident in their clinic, the facility will reach out to the family to arrange for an appointment. Or, the physician may adjust the medication, in which case the nurse will update the records.

With that said, it is fundamental for you and your loved one to understand and know what to expect with the food services before moving into a facility. It's much more than just a meal. Sample the food for yourselves and determine if there are enough varieties and quality in the food service experience to meet your loved one's expectations.

THE TOUR – STATE SURVEY

It is vital that you ask to see the facility's latest state survey results. It's a question that is not asked regularly, because family members aren't familiar with state surveys or may not realize their significance.

Any senior living facility participating in Medicare or Medicaid programs, or regulated by the state, will undergo an annual survey. The state survey is one of, if not the most, prominent events that take place within a facility. The staff and directors spend all year preparing and ensuring documentation is up-to-date and easily accessible.

The survey will determine if the facility is adhering to regulations and operating with current certifications, licenses, and education. Each assisted living facility is required to make readily available the results of their survey, including their deficiencies for infractions against state regulations. Information and descriptions regarding specific codes and laws are available online. After reviewing the facility's results, you'll have the opportunity to research if the infractions were related to abuse and neglect, sanitary and cleanliness, or failed practices. Repeat infractions are a red flag, meaning the facility had not corrected mistakes and additional violations were discovered upon re-survey. If you have specific questions about anything in the survey results, ask the administrator. She or he will be able to explain the situation and provide you with their plan of correction that has been implemented to prevent the issue from happening again. Keep in mind that they must comply with federal HIPPA laws (that protect privacy). The facility is unable to disclose specific details such as which resident was affected or which staff members were involved.

Additionally, some infractions may be minor, such as a record-keeping oversight or a staff member had an expired food handler's permit. Others may be more serious, such as medication errors resulting in the hospitalization of a resident. It's not uncommon to see one or two deficiencies on each survey. A deficiency-free survey is fantastic but rare. As the industry changes and new laws are implemented, it has a sort of ripple effect through the facilities while they update their policies and procedures. It takes a well-informed administrator and health services director who are actively involved with the local healthcare associations and state agencies to receive updates and implement them immediately. Notices of regulation adjustments are sent to facilities via mail and email, and it's up to the administrator to review and make the changes.

During an annual survey, representatives from the state enter the building and meet with the administrator and health services director. They will request particular documents such as the resident roster that includes names and room numbers, and the employee characteristic roster, which lists the employment details for each employee. State survey representatives have full access to records and information within the building.

Signs are posted on the entry doors to inform the public that the facility is undergoing an annual survey. These usually take three or four business days but may be longer if the surveyors discover infractions that require investigating.

The surveyors will review staff records to ensure certificate copies are present and current, and all staff who provide direct care to the residents are credentialed appropriately. They will look to see if the facility is practicing its own policies and procedures, and paperwork is completed with signatures, dates, and filed securely.

Next, they will monitor the kitchen serve-outs and watch for safe food handling. They'll ensure that food products are labeled with the date they were opened and the date they expire. Anyone who enters the kitchen must wash their hands, long hair must be tied back, and staff must wear aprons as a barrier to protect cross contamination from their uniform. Surveyors will observe for respectful and professional interaction between the residents and staff when taking orders and track to see if the food is served in a timely way.

The surveyors will conduct a resident council meeting, in which the staff or administration are not authorized to attend. Residents are encouraged to participate and bring forth any questions, comments, and concerns they may have. The surveyors will ask a series of questions to find out if they are receiving quality care and if they are happy with their facility.

Among other things, the surveyors will also select a few random residents to visit with inside their apartment. This allows for the surveyors to see what condition their homes are in and if they are being maintained for safety and sanitation.

The surveyors will review the nursing department practices, and spend some time looking through medication records, documentation and charting, incident reports, and staff training records. This is a lengthy process, and they will request documentation for any items they find that are not in compliance.

Upon completion of the survey, there will be an exit interview with the administrator and health services director, during which the surveyors will convey any infractions found.

They will identify the regulation code of the infraction and state the issue they found. They will reveal the staff member or the resident involved, and depending on the severity or frequency, they may impose a citation and a fine.

Upon receiving the official report from the state surveyors in the mail, also referred to as a Letter of Deficiencies, the facility will have to come up with a Plan of Action to correct their deficiencies. Once the state surveyors receive the Plan of Action, they schedule a return visit to ensure that all deficiencies have been corrected. If they discover additional infractions during their return visit, they will continue the process until all is back in compliance and the facility receives a clearance.

The official report is then posted within the facility and is available to anyone who wishes to review the document. It will exclude names of residents and staff but will list the issue and the corrective action.

In addition to the state survey results, the fire marshal's report may also be included. Typically, the fire marshal will conduct an inspection before the annual state survey. They look for fire and safety hazards and ensure emergency disaster preparedness. Fire drills should be completed monthly, and contain a training session during each shift – morning, afternoon, and night (referred to as the 'NOC shift'). The frequency may vary by state, but all facilities will be required to hold frequent drills. Emergency evacuation plans must be up to date, and a full evacuation drill should be completed as often as the regulations require. The fire marshal will inspect a few random apartments and look for things such as electric blankets, hot plate warmers, and extension cords without an automatic reset.

It all boils down to the safety of the residents, and with that in mind, the facility should remain diligent in keeping up with the regulations and demands of the state, no matter how troublesome they may seem. Ultimately, there is a reason for implementing such rules. During your search for a facility, look for one that is actively maintaining compliance and correcting their mistakes.

THE TOUR – WRAP UP QUESTIONS

You have met the department heads, visited with some of the residents, and you've toured the facility. Now, it's time to go over any additional questions you may have. There are a few that I encourage you to ask. The answers could be key in the decision-making process. Instead of leaving as soon as the tour is complete, sit down with the admissions coordinator once more and review everything you have been told.

Initially, the financial questions were fairly vague. You may have received a ballpark figure based on the needs of your loved one as you had described them. Now, it's time to dig a little deeper.

Start by asking if any upfront fees are due upon move-in. Does the facility charge a security deposit? Or a community fee? What does this entail, and is it refundable? How about the move-in promotions or discounts? Some facilities may offer sizeable discounts to the rent or fees in an effort to generate traffic and create a sense of urgency. For example, you may hear about an offer to discount the first month's rent if you take possession of the apartment by a certain date.

Next, ask about insurance coverage. Are any of the services covered by insurance, other than Medicaid? Even if you assume the answer, it's always a good idea to check. Third party services are often included, such as physical therapy and occupational therapy. Check if the facility charges any additional fees to establish those services.

Review the services and amenities. This is an opportunity to find out which services are included in the base rental fee and which services require additional funds, or are built into the level of care. Amenities of the apartment and the facility are important to know, as you may need to provide additional household items that are not included and can drive up the cost or skew the budget.

What is the average response time when the resident activates a call-light? Find out if they are staffed appropriately to ensure quick response times for residents, and if there are enough caregivers on the floor to provide quality care for the residents. What is the time window for giving out a scheduled medication? How does the facility handle emergencies that require two staff members to assist with one resident, also known as a two-person-transfer? Depending on the facility and the acuity of care for the residents, the number of caregivers should increase if they have a high volume of residents requiring complex assistance. It is common to hear that a facility is short-staffed. How well do they maintain their staff?

What are the nurse's hours? Do you have someone on-call? What about the weekends, or after hours? Someone qualified to respond to medical emergencies and direct the caregivers should be available at all times, 24/7. In the event of an emergency, the caregivers are trained to respond appropriately, and the nurse and administrator are involved in the process. They are notified of the incident, no matter what time of day. If the caregiver has a question about the situation, he or she will call and speak with the nurse or administrator, who will instruct them through the next step. The nurse is not able to diagnose a medical issue, rather, he or she must communicate to the resident's primary physician to request a medication change, establish certain preventive services, and seek further instructions from the medical professional. As long as the facility has a plan for responding to emergencies and has adequate staff to provide care, you're on the right track.

Next, ask a bit more about dietary services. Does a registered dietician approve the menu? Do they have a dietitian on site?

How do they accommodate special diets? In the event of a diet change ordered by a physician, such as thinned liquids as a result of a stroke, gluten allergy, or perhaps diabetes, the facility may have substitute meals for those in need. Alternatively, the facility may not be equipped to accommodate such diets, and if this is the case, you may need to seek other options.

Does the facility track the meals? Will they be able to tell you if your loved one was in the dining room for lunch today? This is important to know because it will help to stop a potential medical condition from worsening before your loved one ends up in the hospital. When a resident does not consistently come to the dining room for meals, there is usually a medical reason why.

The admissions coordinator may address some of these questions during the tour, but if not, bring a notebook and jot these questions down to prompt you to ask.

If you're not prepared to make a commitment at that time, provide the admissions coordinator with your information and a rough estimate of when you will make your decision. If another party tours and shows interest in the apartment, the facility usually doesn't want to rent it without notifying you first to give you a chance to commit. Seeking assisted living is much more complex than renting a house or apartment in town, and the staff respects that you may need a day or two to make your choice.

Chapter Five

THE DECISION

*Aging is not 'lost youth' but a new stage
of opportunity and strength.*
—Betty Friedan

A FTER YOU'VE TOURED SEVERAL facilities and selected a few that you feel would be suitable for your loved one, and after your loved one has toured the top three facilities, it's time to make a decision.

Contingent on your loved one's cooperative state of mind, it could be a much bigger challenge than simply asking which one they preferred. This type of decision will need to be made sensitively and devoid of aggression or intimidation. Start by setting aside a time to meet with your loved one in their home. Bring all of the necessary literature and notes from the tour and photos of the facility if you have them. You'll want to steer the conversation to enable them to feel in control of the situation. You're just helping to get them from point A to point B. Ask which facility they liked best and why. Discuss which facility would be financially acceptable and will work in the long run, and what to do if they required additional help beyond the assisted living's scope of practice. Gather as much insight as you can and decide together which facility will be the one they'll select.

Let's say Mom is hesitant, and the thought of moving frightens her. Continue to reassure her, and remind her that it's not a move just for pleasure. Instead, it is a necessity. This move is a result of physical challenges and safety concerns, so it's in her best interest to choose the facility while she's got the ability and can get the help she needs.

You may need to be cautious with your word choices. Avoid using phrases or words that will insult or mislead your loved one. The absolute worst thing you can do is lie. It's okay to be creative with your words, in an attempt to redirect a confused and anxious person, but never lie. It can be frustrating at times, but we must remain calm, controlled and persuasive, using facts. If Mom is still resistant to the idea of moving, you may need to employ family members to assist with the conversation.

You can always ask for help from the admissions coordinator or administrator to have this difficult conversation. It's a similar "good-cop, bad-cop" scenario in a sense that you can be the emotional support for your loved one while the professionals lead a discussion about the reasons why it's time to move. Personal experience suggests that my loved ones are less inclined to hear my suggestions, as I'm just "the daughter," but, if a professional reiterates the same thing I had attempted to say, my loved ones are compliant, and do exactly as I had recommended.

Within this conversation of deciding where to move, remember to stay on track. If it's a one-way-street and your loved one is hands-down refusing, then you'll need to lay out a plan so that they understand what could happen next. This plan will need to entail a selected facility so that in the event of an emergency, there will be a place to go. It may appease your loved one, as they'll feel as though they have won and they don't need to move, but in reality, you're laying the foundation for the move. Which facility did you like best? They may be inclined to say "none of them" but rephrase the question and say, "Did you like the facility with the swimming pool or the facility with the beautiful flower garden on the patio?" Discuss amenities and services that are important to your loved one when asking them to choose. As soon as they identify the facility of choice, you can proceed to the next step. Until this selection is made, continue the conversation and discover what will change their mind, and why. Remain persistent, but not aggressive. You could be in for a long conversation, and maybe several attempts at this conversation, but don't give up. You're not the only one dealing with a difficult loved one, and this is all a part of the process. It's not easy to give up independence and a home that has been a comfort zone for decades, but it all boils down to health and safety, and that trumps emotional attachment.

Once the facility has been selected, the next step is conditional to a few things. Do you have a house to sell first, before being able to accept financial responsibility for the apartment? Do you need to tour once more, just to make sure this is the best facility for your loved one? Have you discussed with all family members involved in the decision-making process? Is your loved one still hesitant to go?

Let's say that your loved one still has some reservations and is not confident with the decision to move. There is a solution that worked for many of my residents and made the transition much less stressful. They took advantage of a respite stay within the facility, to try it out first. A respite stay is a short-term—usually less than 30 days—retreat, much like a resort stay. The facility will furnish an apartment and provide all of the services needed during that temporary stay so that the resident can get a feel for what it's like and squash all stereotypes about assisted living. They will meet the staff and other residents and enjoy the meals provided by the facility. They can acclimate to the relaxing atmosphere, try a few activities, and see what life is like within a facility before committing to move in. It's a creative way to enable your loved one to remain in control of the decision-making process, and it doesn't make them feel like they're trapped. I've had many successful move-ins as a result of this non-pressure method, and the resident had enough time to switch their mindset to be more accepting of assisted living. They liked being welcomed, and thoroughly enjoyed visiting with others who went through the same transition. They received support from those who understood what the resident was feeling.

Respite stay apartments may not be available in all facilities, so be sure to check and see if they offer this feature.

THE NEXT STEP – RESERVATION DEPOSIT

Your loved one has selected a facility and is agreeable to moving. There may not be a target move-in date yet, but that's okay, we'll get to that. The next order of business should be a trip to the facility with a reservation deposit in hand. Most facilities will require a deposit to hold an apartment until your loved one is ready to move. Generally speaking, the reservation deposit likely won't guarantee an apartment; however, it will give you the first right of refusal. To break it down, let's say you place a deposit on an apartment to hold it while you finish some business before moving Mom in. Maybe she's recovering from an illness in the hospital and will need a few weeks of rehabilitation in the skilled nursing center before she's ready for assisted living. You want to secure a place for her to go once she's recovered. The assisted living facility may hold the apartment until someone else comes along and wants to move into that unit. If that's the case, the admissions coordinator will call you and say they've got someone who is interested in renting the apartment you reserved. If you don't want to miss out on this particular apartment, you'll need to accept financial responsibility. Or, if you're not ready and cannot begin to pay rent on the apartment, you could refuse and remain on the list to be contacted for the next available unit. As a reminder, the facilities are census driven, so they will be calling and pushing for that financial commitment.

Ask the admissions coordinator if they have any move-in specials, or if they can waive a fee to help ease the financial burden. Most of the time, they will negotiate with you and work out an arrangement to get your financial commitment. I used to offer a discounted rent rate for a couple of weeks while the new resident finished their rehabilitation stay, as they were paying for the rent there in addition to the assisted living. It was something of value that I could offer in exchange for a commitment for the apartment, which would pay off in the long run. The assisted living facility should do what they can to help. Typically, the larger the corporation, the more flexibility they have. This is a bold statement, but generally speaking, it's true. Of course, there may be dynamics that invalidate my point, but truly, these facilities should have a little wiggle room.

The reservation deposit could have some contingencies, so find out what they are. Is the deposit refundable? Do they apply it toward the rent? What happens to the deposit if things don't work out, and your loved one moves out? Each facility is different, so check into it before making the commitment.

PHYSICIAN ORDERS

After the reservation deposit is collected by the facility, the next step of the move-in process is for the facility to obtain physician orders from your loved one's primary doctor. Actually, there are several steps that happen simultaneously, so for simplicity, we'll review the most important ones first.

Physician orders, or doctor's orders, must be obtained prior to moving in. They are, essentially, a prescription for assisted living. Some facilities will have a packet of paperwork ready to send to the doctor's office, and they'll need your loved one to sign an authorization form to release medical information to the facility.

Additionally, they'll gather some basic and demographical information such as birth date, Social Security number, insurance information, and emergency contacts. The facility's admissions coordinator or nurse will fax the request for physician orders to the doctor with a note stating that they're anticipating a mutual client to move into the facility on a particular date. If your loved one has not been to the clinic in a while, the doctor may require an appointment for him or her to come in and be checked out first. The facility will follow up with the clinic if the orders are not received within a few days. Normally, the physician's office will contact the person in charge of scheduling an appointment, but it's important to follow up to avoid delays.

Physician orders are the golden ticket to staying in an assisted living facility. Without a doctor's signature stating that the resident has a medical diagnosis and requires the services, that resident cannot stay within the facility. If a resident moves in without signed physician orders, the facility could face disciplinary actions from the state for providing care to a resident without direction from a physician. Some doctors are difficult to get a response from and may take a long time to complete the paperwork. Occasionally, it takes the teamwork of the nurse or admissions coordinator along with the family member to call the doctor's office and request the orders as soon as possible. Sometimes, it may seem like the facility is annoyingly persistent with their phone calls to the office in hopes to get the orders signed and returned as soon as possible. Doctors are tremendously busy, but they also understand the importance of paperwork to get their mutual client into a safe environment. The admissions coordinator may drop off cookies or a gift at your loved one's clinic to express gratitude and to maintain the professional relationship.

HEALTH ASSESSMENT & SERVICE PLAN

The nurse will complete an assessment to determine the specific needs of the resident and to establish a baseline for the medical conditions. This step may have been completed prior to the move-in process as a pre-screen to determine if your loved one was suitable for assisted living. If so, they may need only a few additional items to narrow down an accurate level of care determination. Some facilities will require your loved one to visit the nurse in the office, and others may offer to complete the assessment at your loved one's home. Either way, this process doesn't take too long, and the nurse will check from head to toe for things such as swelling in the feet and legs for edema. The nurse will gather vitals such as blood pressure, weight, and other basic health information to use as a baseline.

Once the assessment is complete, the nurse will put together a service plan and coordinate the services required. You or your loved one will need to review the completed service plan and most likely sign to acknowledge the services to be provided.

PAPERWORK

In-house paperwork will be completed next, which includes the rental agreement, policies and procedures, resident rights, and HIPPA forms. The admissions coordinator will collect copies of insurance cards and long-term care policies.

They will request that you bring along the original POLST (Physician Orders for Life-Sustaining Treatment) form or advance directives. This will enable the staff or emergency personnel to accommodate your loved one's wishes in the event of a life-threatening medical emergency. Some residents do not wish to be resuscitated, and if so, the facility must have the proper forms in place, and they must be signed by both the resident and their physician. The original form is kept in the resident's medical chart, and a copy is placed on their refrigerator inside their apartment. During an emergency, the first responders will look for the POLST behind the door or on the fridge, and if it is not present within those precious few seconds upon arrival, they will begin life-saving measures. If your loved one does not have this form, you will need to schedule an appointment with the primary care physician, during which the doctor will discuss the options, and your loved one will decide his or her wishes. Again, the POLST or advance directives must be signed by a physician and your loved one to be valid.

NOW WHAT?

Paperwork is done, the physician orders were signed and returned, and you're ready to go. The admissions coordinator will give you the keys, and you'll get the green light to move personal belongings into the apartment. At this time, a target move-in date is established so that the staff can be prepared with the correct medications and dosages, and ensure that someone will be ready to provide your loved one with an official orientation. Most facilities will discourage move-ins during the weekend, as the nurse and department head staff would not be there to assist with the transition. Additionally, most physician offices are closed over the weekend and cannot provide answers or orders if there are issues with the medications. It's highly recommended to choose a move-in date during the week and in the morning.

Another reminder while you bring furniture into the apartment and begin to set it up; be sure to watch for potential trip hazards and clutter. If there's a table with lots of fragile items on it, they could get broken if your loved one stumbles and reaches for the table to steady themselves. Rugs are not recommended anywhere, and a clear path to the recliner or couch is a must. It's going to be hard to choose which piece of furniture can stay and which can go, but safety is more important than a bookshelf or a chair. Sometimes it's best not to have your loved one present as you move in the furniture, as it may become stressful and cause anxiety for them. This is a case-by-case situation, and you know your loved one best. If you think Dad won't worry and he's excited to move, then by all means, he should be present. If you recognize that he's a bit anxious and unsure, then keep him occupied at home while the apartment is getting set up. In a way, it's much easier to use your best judgment and determine where to safely place the furniture without feeling guilty about how it makes your loved one feel to see some of that furniture removed.

It's *always* about safety. Remain sensitive, but also sensible.

Chapter Six

READY TO GO

Age is an issue of mind over matter.
If you don't mind, it doesn't matter.
—Mark Twain

*I*T'S MOVE-IN DAY! LET'S VISUALIZE a typical scenario: Mom walks through the front doors of the facility and is greeted by the receptionist and other residents. The department head staff come out of their offices and greet her, offering coffee or a snack before she goes to the apartment. You head over to the elevator with Mom, who is waving, smiling and greeting the other residents as they say hello back.

Even though your stomach is in knots, you should feel a sense of relief. All of the hard work is done, and you've accomplished your primary goal: to get your loved one into a safe environment where she will be cared for properly, to enhance her quality of life.

Moving day can bring a wealth of emotions to you both. It's something that needs to be prepared for, both mentally and physically. Remind your loved one that this is not just a change of address; it's an enhancement to their lifestyle. Do so by talking about the highlights of what she can expect, and the positive impacts it will have. It works best to get her excited for the move. Believe it or not, your loved one will be a little eager to see what's in store for them. Even if Mom doesn't show it, she's glad to be getting some help and the medical attention she so badly needed.

You'll want to make sure to update and forward your loved one's mail to the new location as well as billing addresses and other services. Common updates include banking profile, telephone service, and cable TV (which may already be provided by the facility as an included service).

Check with the admissions coordinator to see if basic toiletries are included in the rent. Depending on the state where you live, and whether your loved one is on Medicaid, some items such as toilet paper, toothpaste, and body wash could be provided. If not, you'll want to bring those along with you.

In your loved one's apartment, all pull cords or call-light stations must be kept clear and accessible at all times. The facility will have random audits from an outside agency to ensure that each station is in compliance, or the facility could face fines, or lose funding. If your loved one has a cognitive impairment and won't remember to pull the call-light when he or she needs help, there are a few interventions to fix the situation. Ask the staff to provide a brightly colored sign that says something like "Pull Cord for Help" and tape it above each call-light station. If the facility is equipped with pendants in addition to the call-lights, that would be the preferred route. Pendants are useful because the resident can wear the button around their neck. In the event of a fall and they cannot reach the call-light, they can push the button on the necklace and help will arrive.

One more thing about move-in day. Be mindful that the move may set your loved one back cognitively. Usually this is temporary and they are pleasantly confused for the first thirty days while they're getting oriented to their new surroundings. As much as we don't want to admit it, your loved one will not be themselves for the first little while. Many residents will often call their families and embellish stories of how terrible the service has been, or that they didn't get any dinner when, in fact, they refused when offered. It's an odd way for the resident to reach out to their families and either impress guilt or seek sympathy as a method of coping with their new environment and feelings toward the changes. Always look into it and never disregard, as they could be telling the truth. But also remember, it's best not to react with emotions that could upset your loved one more. Instead, remain calm and reassure her that you will check into her complaint, and notify the appropriate person in the facility to verify that all is well. Many of the complaints from residents stem from their confusion and impaired cognitive ability to problem solve.

THINGS THAT GOOGLE WON'T TELL YOU

There are a few things you and your loved one should know while moving into a facility, and understand the boundaries of an assisted living facility's scope of practice.

First and foremost; know that it is not a one-on-one caregiving situation. This is a facility with other residents who have similar medical complications and require a variety of services. The staff will do their best to respond to calls promptly, but there may be a delay or inconsistency with response times. In a facility with forty-four apartments and three caregivers working during a shift, the average response time for a call should be an average of three to four minutes after a call-light button is pressed. If there is an emergency with another resident, the response may be delayed.

Of course, it is unacceptable for a facility to be staffed inadequately and struggle to respond to a call-light, but it does happen in some places. If you were to interview ten caregivers from any facility, the chances are likely that they'll tell you they feel understaffed and overworked. Failure to respond to a resident's needs could trigger an investigation from the state, if reported. It could even classify as resident abuse. If you suspect any form of abuse or neglect, I strongly suggest that you report it immediately to your state hotline. The National Adult Protective Services Association's website can direct you to a local phone number to report a case.

CHECK-IN

During the check-in, bring all current medications and give them to the nurse. She will verify the medications and their dosages with the med-list provided by your loved one's primary care physician. If something does not match or is not listed on the medication list, the nurse will not be able to use the medication, and it will be returned to you. If there is a medication that is listed and you have not provided it, the nurse will fax the pharmacy for a refill. Some states require medications to be bubble-packed or packaged in individual doses, rather than in a pill bottle. If so, the nurse will communicate this with you and fax the pharmacy for a refill in the required packaged form. The important thing to remember when checking in the prescriptions is to be patient and understand that the facility must follow the policies and procedures to remain in compliance with state law. This can be frustrating, especially if it requires you to make a trip to the pharmacy or if the nurse cannot use an expensive bottle of pills because it's the wrong dosage. They will sort things out and communicate with both you and the physician to ensure everything matches per physician order, which will avoid medication errors.

DAY ONE

It's the first day, and Mom spent the night in her apartment. Hopefully, she woke up feeling refreshed and comfortable, but it's possible that she didn't get much sleep. This is normal, and as she acclimates, she'll begin to relax.

If possible, visit your loved one in the morning or have breakfast in the dining room with them. It helps with the transition to know that you haven't simply "dumped" them. Unfortunately, there are cases in which this happens. It's heartbreaking to meet a brand-new resident in the facility with stress and anxiety across written across their face as they hold it all in, without an outlet or someone familiar to visit with. I've built relationships with so many residents who became like my own family member. Many have since passed away, and the feelings of sadness are crippling after every loss. The residents become a part of the assisted living family after they move into a facility, and the staff genuinely cares for them.

Later in the evening, after you've gone home and Mom continues to get settled, give her a call and encourage her to go to all of the meals the next day and participate in the activities. It may be intimidating for her at first, but the staff will pair her up with someone who will be a suitable companion and share similar interests. If Mom is too anxious, emotional, and stressed, it's not a bad idea to support her desire to stay in her apartment and have her meals delivered, but this should be a last resort. Having support from family is a crucial factor to a successful transition, so try to be there as often as possible within the first week.

During this first day, Mom will be greeted by all staff during each shift, and she'll be given an official orientation to the building. If she has any questions, the staff will answer them and offer additional insight into what she can expect. Mom will be notified of her schedule for showers, laundry, and housekeeping, if pre-determined in the level of care.

The activity director will spend extra time with the newest member of the facility and encourage participation during the activities. They will promote friendships with other residents, perhaps by hosting coffee socials and special events to introduce the new resident to the others. This is an effective way to reduce stress and make a new resident feel welcome. The activity director will find out what type of activities are of special interest and may attempt to create a special activity just for them. Before you know it, your loved one is in the activity room, and she has joined the facility Wii bowling league.

THE FIRST MONTH

The first thirty days are the "honeymoon," during which the staff is getting to know the resident, and what their routine preferences are, and vice versa. The service plan will detail what services are needed, and the staff will get to know behavioral inclinations, such as a shower late in the evening or early in the morning; or, if the resident likes to have a cup of coffee before getting dressed and ready for the day, or, if they prefer to read the newspaper at their table in the facility dining room instead of in their apartment. All of these things will be discovered and implemented accordingly, as the schedule allows. On occasion, there may be a day in which the resident will not receive their shower at their desired time, and this usually causes an upset in the routine. Staff members do everything in their power to avoid such upsets in the routine.

After the first month, you may notice that Mom is cognitively sharper than the first day she moved in, and she may seem more relaxed. By now, she's made some friends, participated in activities, and she'll have their own spot in the dining room and regularly visits with her table mates. She'll spend time outside of the apartment in the common area with other residents. Mom will have learned many of the names of staff members, and their apartment will feel much like home again. This is when you can breathe a sigh of relief, and know that she's safe.

Conclusion

THE DESTINATION

To reach a port we must sail,
sometimes with the wind, and sometimes against it.
But we must not drift or lie at anchor.
—Oliver Wendell Holmes, Sr.

CONGRATULATIONS! IF YOU'VE REACHED this part of the journey, then you have arrived at your destination. You have accomplished something that you thought would be impossible, but guided direction and knowledge of what to expect have brought you to this point.

Your situation may be different from others, but the line from point A to point B, or unsafe to safe, is the same. You've dealt with behaviors and heartache, guilt and regret, and hopefully, you can forgive those feelings and celebrate that you've successfully enhanced your loved one's quality of life.

In turn, they may live longer and happier. You're no longer burdened with being a caretaker and make difficult decisions.

As the family member, you will remain involved and continue to have to make decisions with health issues as they come up, but you've got a team of professionals who can provide knowledgeable support and assistance in the process.

If you're still feeling uneasy about your decision, know that it takes time to adjust. There are so many other sons and daughters, brothers and sisters, grandchildren and spouses who are feeling as if they could have done more. These feelings are normal, but you must remind yourself what initially started this process, and why it's in your loved one's best interest to be in a safe environment.

If it's financial guilt, worry not. You cannot put a price on safety. If it's emotional guilt for uprooting your loved one from a place they had been for so long; again, do not fret. You made the right choice. It's because of you that your loved one is getting the proper care as they deserve.

Everyone ages differently, some more gracefully than others. Whether it be cognitive or physical challenges or both, they present different issues and are alleviated by getting into a safe environment. The journey of moving into assisted living will depend on those challenges, and local resources and professionals can help. You know your loved one best, but sometimes it takes the skill of a specialist to say what needs to be said and guide you to do what needs to be done.

Nobody truly desires to be in an assisted living facility. If we had the power, we would all live out our days in the comfort of our home, surrounded by our family. But we cannot predict or change what our future brings. We can only accept it as it comes and work hard to ensure that our choices are in the best interest of those we love. Even if it means a few tears shed or harsh words are spoken from them, remember that their declining condition and their physical challenges cause these changes in personality, and they do not love you any less than before.

It's hard to bear the responsibility of taking care of someone else, but once we've been put into that position and we have accepted that responsibility, we must set aside our emotions and act upon logic and reasoning.

There are many support groups out there, no matter where you live. If the challenge becomes too much to bear, then please reach out, and someone can help. You do not have to endure this alone, and there are several avenues that can be taken to accomplish the goal of getting your loved one into a senior living community.

Life is spontaneous and unpredictable. Worrying about something we don't have any power over creates stress, anxiety, and heartache. Instead, we can change the direction of our sails and the path to our destination becomes ours to navigate.

Now, let's get busy living life to the fullest.

Common Abbreviations

Common Abbreviations In
Senior Living Communities

ALF – Assisted Living Facility

SNF – Skilled Nursing Facility

IL – Independent Living

AFH – Adult Family Home

CCRC – Continuing Care Retirement Communities

ADL – Activities of Daily Living

LOC – Level of Care

MCD – Medicaid

MCA - Medicare

PCA – Personal Care Attendant

CNA – Certified Nursing Assistant

LPN – Licensed Practical Nurse

RN – Registered Nurse

UTI – Urinary Tract Infection

POLST – Provider Orders for Life-Sustaining Treatment

Resources

National Adult Protective Services Association: NAPSA

www.napsa-now.org

National Long-Term Care Ombudsman Resource Center

https://Itcombudsman.org

National Medicaid / CMS Headquarters

https://www.medicaid.gov/about-us/contact-us/index.html

National Medicare

1-800-MEDICARE

National Center for Assisted Living: NCAL

https://www.ahcancal.org/ncal/Pages/index.aspx

Thank You!

To My Readers

I am profoundly humbled and forever grateful to everyone who has purchased my book and taken the time out of your day to read it. I hope I was able to provide some helpful insight and assist you along the way.

Thank you to those who recommend my book to your friends, and continue to spread the word. I don't represent a senior living company; this book was written from my heart to fulfill my desire to help others.

Thank you so much to everyone who reviews my book. There is no greater gift to an author.